Dream Big Dreams

PHOTOGRAPHS FROM
BARACK OBAMA'S
INSPIRING AND
HISTORIC PRESIDENCY

★ ★ ★

A BOOK FOR YOUNG READERS BY
PETE SOUZA
FORMER CHIEF OFFICIAL
WHITE HOUSE PHOTOGRAPHER

LITTLE, BROWN AND COMPANY
New York Boston

The American Recovery and Reinvestment Act, also known as the stimulus package. The U.S. economy was in a tailspin and this major piece of legislation, signed less than a month after President Obama took office, helped set things back on track.

FEBRUARY 17, 2009

Contents

It is you, the young and fearless at heart,
the most diverse and educated generation in our history,
who the nation is waiting to follow.

— Barack Obama

Introduction

★ ★ ★

The job of the Chief Official White House Photographer is to visually document the President of the United States for history. Sounds simple. But *what* and *how much* you photograph depends on each chief photographer and his or her relationship with the President.

I had already established a professional relationship with Barack Obama years before he was elected President. As the national photographer for the *Chicago Tribune,* I spent hundreds of hours documenting his rise to power as a U.S. Senator beginning in early 2005.

Four years later, he asked me to become his White House photographer. Knowing each other's work habits and personality made for a somewhat seamless transition. I also knew the inner workings of 1600 Pennsylvania Avenue—the White House—since I had worked there as a White House photographer for President Ronald Reagan.

Starting on Inauguration Day, January 20, 2009, I was determined to create the best photographic archive of a President that had ever been done. That meant I needed to always be around. Every day. Or to borrow a line from Lin-Manuel Miranda's musical *Hamilton,* my goal was to always be in "the room where it happens."

My job sounds cool: hang around with the President and take pictures. But it was really hard. Physically. Mentally. Spiritually. It is a job meant for someone with some photographic and life experience, yet some youth and energy. Ideally someone in their mid-30s, maybe early 40s, tops. I started the job when I was 54.

Someone once described working at the White House as trying to take a sip of water from a fire hose that never shuts off. That's a pretty good analogy. Just when you think you have a break, *boom*, you realize that documenting the President for history is an all-consuming, 24/7, always-on-call, no-vacation, no-sick-days, smartphone-always-vibrating kind of job.

President Obama and I shared a lot of time in each other's presence. Probably more than anyone else except for his family. Ten to 12 hours a day. Five days a week, sometimes six or seven. Photographing every meeting, every day. In the Oval Office, the Situation Room, the Roosevelt Room. And then on the road. Nearly 1.5 million miles on *Air Force One*. All 50 states; more than 60 countries. Two million photographs in eight years.

Along the way, I became his friend. And he became my friend. How could you not when you spend so much time together? Did I get on his nerves? Certainly. Did he get on my nerves? One learns to always say no.

In the 12 years that I've known Barack Obama, the character of this man has not changed that much, if at all. Deep down, the core of him is the same. He often tells his daughters, "Be kind and be useful." That shows you a lot about him. As a man. A father. A husband. And a President of the United States.

This book represents some of the moments I captured of President Obama throughout his Presidency. The big moments and the small moments. Fun moments. Moments during a crisis. Moments of laughter. Moments when I was hiding tears behind the viewfinder. Intimate family moments. Symbolic moments and, yes, historic moments.

I have had the extraordinary privilege of being the person in the room for eight years, visually documenting President Obama for history. I hope you will see in my photographs the same honor and integrity of this man that I witnessed every day.

Running into his daughters, Malia and Sasha, on the Colonnade after they had returned home from school one afternoon.

MARCH 5, 2009

Be Kind and Respectful

★ ★ ★

Words do matter. Actions mean more. President Obama may have told his daughters to "be kind and be useful." But more important was the way he conducted himself in his daily interactions with others. I witnessed this whether he was greeting Pope Francis in the Oval Office, fist-bumping a custodian in the White House complex, or greeting a young Syrian refugee overseas. These moments exemplified a President who treated every person with kindness and respect.

Talking with a young girl at an educational center for refugees in Kuala Lumpur, Malaysia. President Obama was in the country to attend Asia summit meetings with world leaders. He stopped by the classroom to highlight his call for more kindness and empathy in dealing with the global refugee crisis.

NOVEMBER 21, 2015

President Obama adjusts the tie of Patrick Phy, 5, before a ceremony for his father, Coast Guard Military Aide Commander Scott S. Phy. The President wanted to make sure that Patrick looked good for their family photo.
JUNE 12, 2014

Greeting a young performer at the Cannon Ball Flag Day Powwow during his visit to the Standing Rock Sioux Reservation in Cannon Ball, North Dakota. It was only the fourth visit to an Indian reservation by a President of the United States. According to the *Washington Post*, many tribal leaders said that Obama did more for Native Americans than all of his predecessors combined.

JUNE 13, 2014

President Obama talks to a young woman during an unannounced visit to the Boys and Girls Clubs in Cleveland, Ohio. She was visibly nervous in his presence, so he spent a few minutes trying to make her feel comfortable.

JUNE 14, 2012

★ 13

With Pope Francis after their meeting in the Oval Office. Moments later, the President introduced the Pope to two of his personal aides, Ferial Govashiri and Brian Mosteller. Each told me later it was one of the best moments—and kindest gestures by the President—during their eight years working in the administration.

SEPTEMBER 23, 2015

A traditional greeting with His Holiness the 14th Dalai Lama in the Map Room of the White House. The President respected the exiled Tibetan leader and met with him four times during his Presidency despite objection from the leaders of China, who felt the Dalai Lama supported separating Tibet from China.

FEBRUARY 21, 2014

Having a green tea ice cream bar with his hosts at the Great Buddha of Kamakura, Japan. The President later told me he had visited this same Buddha as a child and remembered sitting in the same place, eating the same kind of ice cream.

NOVEMBER 14, 2010

Greeting villagers along Main Street in Moneygall, Ireland.
President Obama enjoyed being able to meet people from all
walks of life on his many trips abroad.

MAY 23, 2011

A fist-bump with a boy who was trying to greet the President from behind a door locked for security purposes in the Cidade de Deus favela in Rio de Janeiro, Brazil. President Obama was walking into the community to wave at the many people gathered and heard the boy shouting excitedly from behind the locked door.

MARCH 20, 2011

The President always made sure to acknowledge everyday workers.

Fist-bumping Larry Lipscomb, a General Services Administration worker, following a White House forum on jobs and economic growth, in the Eisenhower Executive Office Building. The GSA, an independent agency of the U.S. government, was established in 1949 to help manage and support the basic functioning of federal agencies.

DECEMBER 3, 2009

Meeting vendor Saied E. Abedy while walking back to the
White House from a coffee shop in Washington. **JUNE 9, 2014**

Greeting a kitchen worker at El Mago de las Fritas
restaurant in Miami, Florida. **OCTOBER 11, 2010**

Work Hard

★ ★ ★

Being the President of the United States is more than a nine-to-five job. Yes, President Obama spent many hours in meetings during the day. But he was always on call, every minute of every day for eight years. I often photographed him working on the weekend or even while he was on vacation with his family. He was also very disciplined about making productive use of his limited time during the day when no one was with him—reading or writing in the Oval Office in between meetings. Every night after dinner with his family, he would work alone in the Treaty Room, his office in the private residence, until well past midnight.

Working at the Resolute Desk in the Oval Office. The desk was a gift from Queen Victoria to President Rutherford B. Hayes in 1880, and has been used by many Presidents in the Oval Office.

OCTOBER 18, 2013

★ 23

Editing a speech with Jon Favreau, his chief speechwriter at the time. The President liked to work collaboratively with the speechwriters, oftentimes taking hours to rewrite and edit a draft, and then going over each change in person with the speechwriter.

SEPTEMBER 9, 2009

Working on his final State of the Union address with chief speechwriter Cody Keenan. This annual speech was always one of the most important of the year, and the process of writing often took weeks and sometimes months. This was one of the last drafts of the speech, which he delivered later that night.

JANUARY 12, 2016

With President Vladimir Putin of Russia following a lunch with
other foreign leaders in Normandy, France. Though the lunch itself was a
ceremonial event, this conversation showed the President had to always
be ready to talk with our adversaries in a meaningful way. It was the first
time the two had met after months of tension because of Russia's
annexation of Crimea and alleged involvement in the violence in Ukraine.

JUNE 6, 2014

Monitoring the mission with his National Security team to capture or kill Osama bin Laden, who had masterminded the 9/11 terrorist attacks on our country. Though these were the most powerful people in our government, anxiety and tension showed on their faces because they had already made their decision to launch this special-operations mission, and now all they could do was watch from afar.

MAY 1, 2011

★ 27

A plaque on the Resolute Desk given to the President by senior advisor David Axelrod, who made the phrase a refrain during the efforts to pass health care reform. The Affordable Care Act, which was passed in 2010, was the first time a President had been able to pass a bill to help millions of people acquire health insurance.

JANUARY 29, 2016

Talking with President Lee Myung-bak of South Korea at 11:00 p.m. in the Treaty Room.
North Korea had just conducted an artillery attack against the South Korean island of Yeonpyeong.

Aboard *Marine One* (the President's helicopter), flying over the Gulf Coast, the President talks with Louisiana Governor Bobby Jindal and Commander Thad Allen about the BP oil spill. The President and his administration often had to deal with unexpected man-made and natural disasters.

MAY 2, 2010

Discussing a statement about the protests in Ferguson, Missouri, with Deputy National Security Advisor Ben Rhodes, left, and Attorney General Eric Holder. A white police officer had shot Michael Brown, an unarmed black teenager, which caused simmering racial tensions to boil over. The President was on vacation in Martha's Vineyard, Massachusetts.

AUGUST 14, 2014

Talking on the phone with a Democratic Congressman two nights before the final vote in Congress for the Affordable Care Act. The President was trying to convince the wavering Congressman to vote in favor of the bill that would help provide health insurance for millions of people currently not covered. It was the culmination of nearly a year of work.

MARCH 19, 2010

Make Time for Family

★ ★ ★

Like any parent, President Obama would attend his daughters' school recitals and sports activities. For a while, he convened Sunday basketball clinics for the girls and their friends. He also always made time for his wife, Michelle. If she or one of the girls stopped by the Oval Office to see him, he would interrupt whatever he was doing. Though he was considered the most powerful person in the world, he was still a husband and dad first, and proved that by spending quality time with his family every day.

The President and First Lady pose for a family portrait in the Rose Garden on Easter Sunday. With Malia, 16, left, and Sasha, 13, right, along with their dogs, Sunny, left, and Bo.

APRIL 5, 2010

Relaxing with the family in the Oval Office after the girls had returned home from school one afternoon. They had only lived at the White House for two weeks, so the family was still adjusting to their new temporary home.

FEBRUARY 2, 2009

Playing with Sasha and Malia in the Rose Garden during a Saturday break because of a massive snowstorm. I had spent the previous night in my office, knowing that it would be difficult to drive to the White House after the storm, and I suspected that he and the girls might play in the snow.

FEBRUARY 6, 2010

Cuddling with Sasha during a celebration in honor of his 49th birthday. Although dozens of guests had been invited to the outdoor barbecue, he still found time to spend a few moments with each of his daughters.

AUGUST 7, 2010

Chatting with Malia in the midst of the BP oil spill crisis. The President had been working in the Oval Office and spotted Malia sitting alone on the swing set. So he wandered outside for a few minutes to talk with her.

MAY 4, 2010

Helping Malia and Sasha with their shooting skills. Basketball was
his sport of choice, and when the girls joined their school teams, he
began holding Sunday afternoon clinics for the girls and their friends.
MARCH 4, 2012

Horsing around with Malia and Sasha after "A Celebration of the
Music of Broadway" performance at the White House.

JULY 19, 2010

With the First Lady, gazing at the Chicago skyline from the shore of Lake Michigan. Michelle Obama grew up on the South Side of the city, and it became the President's adopted hometown after college. For the two of them, Chicago was where their life together began.

JUNE 15, 2012

Having fun with Sasha during a family dinner on the roof of the Ritz-Carlton
hotel in Moscow, Russia. The First Lady and Malia are at left. Marian Robinson
(in red), Michelle's mother, and Kaye Wilson, the girls' godmother, are at right.
JULY 7, 2009

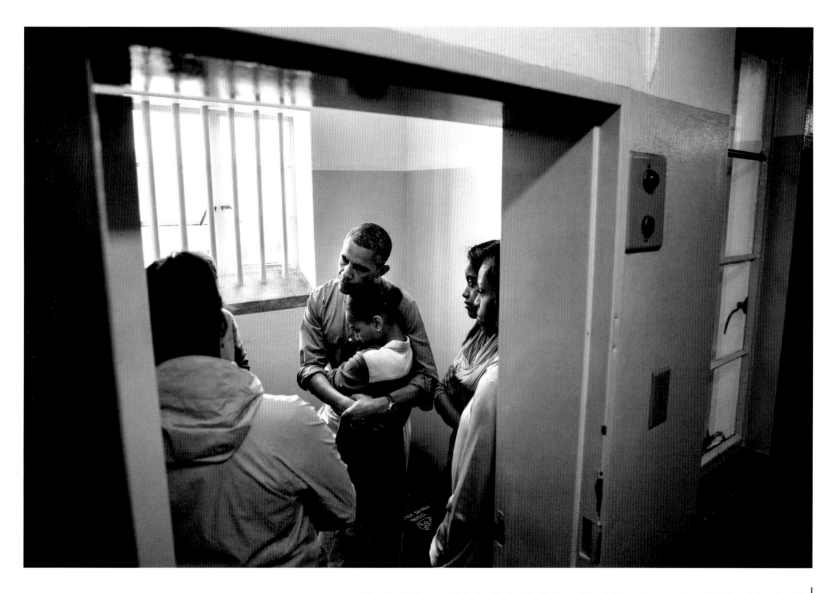

The President and his family inside Nelson Mandela's prison cell on Robben Island, off Cape Town, South Africa. Sasha hugged her father as they listened to one of Mandela's former prison mates talk about his experience there. Mandela was imprisoned for 27 years before apartheid (institutional racial segregation and discrimination) ended; he became the first President of South Africa to be elected by a fully free and democratic process.

JUNE 30, 2013

Watching on television with the girls as the First Lady delivered
her speech at the Democratic National Convention.
SEPTEMBER 4, 2012

Malia had stopped by to see her dad after school, and as they were chatting in the Oval Office, she noticed something on his face and wiped it off.

FEBRUARY 23, 2015

★ 47

Malia and Sasha walking along the Cross Hall on the State Floor of the White House with their parents, Canadian Prime Minister Justin Trudeau, and his wife, Sophie, during a state dinner. The girls had never attended a state dinner as guests and the Obamas thought it would be nice if they went to one before his Presidency ended.

MARCH 10, 2016

Show Compassion

★ ★ ★

President Obama showed his compassion to friends and newcomers alike every day. It was a trait that seemingly came natural to him. Too many times, I photographed him as our consoler in chief, comforting families directly affected by a national tragedy. He felt it was his obligation, on behalf of the country. As our commander in chief, he also regularly visited members of the military who had been injured in service to our country. Whether hugging someone in distress or whispering a few words to ease their pain, his compassion made him a respected President of the United States and a role model for future young leaders.

President Obama writes a school excuse note for Alanah Poullard, 5, while visiting with Wounded Warriors and their families in the East Room during their tour of the White House. Alanah asked for a note to show her kindergarten teacher on why she had missed school.

SEPTEMBER 19, 2013

Visiting with Alex Myteberi, 6, and his family. Alex wrote to the President after seeing a heartbreaking photograph of Syrian boy Omran Daqneesh covered in blood and dust after an air strike: "Can you please go get him and bring him to my home...." he wrote. "We will give him a family and he will be our brother." The President read ten letters a night, five days a week for eight years, that his correspondence office chose as particularly representative but also sometimes very emotional. This letter struck a chord with the President so much that he read parts of it during a speech at the United Nations and then invited Alex's family to the White House.

NOVEMBER 10, 2016

President Obama greets guests following a ceremony honoring those who lost their lives and to commemorate the tenth anniversary of the 9/11 terrorist attacks at the Flight 93 National Memorial in Shanksville, Pennsylvania. Earlier that day, the President and First Lady visited the 9/11 Memorial in New York; later that day, they visited the Pentagon Memorial. The 9/11 attacks were the worst in our nation's history, with almost 3,000 people killed.

SEPTEMBER 11, 2011

A few days after the bin Laden raid, President Obama traveled to New York City and toasted firefighters during a lunch at Engine 54, Ladder 4, Battalion 9 Firehouse. The firehouse, known as the Pride of Midtown, lost 15 firefighters on 9/11—an entire shift, more than any other New York firehouse.

MAY 5, 2011

President Obama meets with Damien and Glenda Moore at a local Federal Emergency Management Agency (FEMA) Disaster Recovery Center tent in Staten Island, New York. The Moores' two small children, Brandon and Connor, died after being swept away when Glenda's car stalled in rising flood waters during Hurricane Sandy while trying to evacuate from Staten Island. The President knew their story and had asked to meet them.

NOVEMBER 15, 2012

Meeting Hugh Hills, 85, in front of his home in Joplin, Missouri, several days after an F5 tornado devastated the city and caused more than 150 fatalities and more than 1,000 injuries. Hills hid in a closet during the tornado, which destroyed the second floor and half the first floor of his house.

MAY 29, 2011

Throughout his administration, President Obama made regular visits to wounded members of the U.S. armed services at Walter Reed Hospital in suburban Washington. The tenth patient he visited on February 28, 2010, did not look at all familiar to me. His name was Cory Remsburg. He had suffered a severe brain injury caused by a roadside explosion in Afghanistan.

The President was told that he had previously met Cory in Normandy in June 2009. I had no immediate remembrance of that encounter. As the President presented him with a Presidential coin (top right), it wasn't clear that Cory could fully understand what the President was saying to him.

Cory's family asked the President if he could sign a photograph that was hanging in the hospital room. And there it was: a photograph that I had taken that day, eight months ago, of Army Ranger Cory Remsburg firmly shaking the hand of President Obama. I was stunned as I looked at the photograph that I had taken on June 6, 2009 (above).

My mind raced back in time. June 6 had been a whirlwind day in France. We'd had an event with U.S. embassy personnel in Paris; a flight on *Air Force One* from Paris to Caen; a state visit with President Nicolas Sarkozy of France; a picturesque helicopter ride into Normandy; the 65th anniversary of D-Day; a helicopter ride, then a plane ride back to Paris; and finally, a tour with the Obama family at the Notre Dame Cathedral. The President and First Lady greeted hundreds of people that day, including a small group of Army Rangers in Normandy.

"God bless…" the President began his inscription on the photo.

Although Cory was severely injured, less than four years later he stood in uniform as an honored guest of the President at the State of the Union address. The following year, the President stopped by his new house outside of Phoenix, Arizona (bottom right).

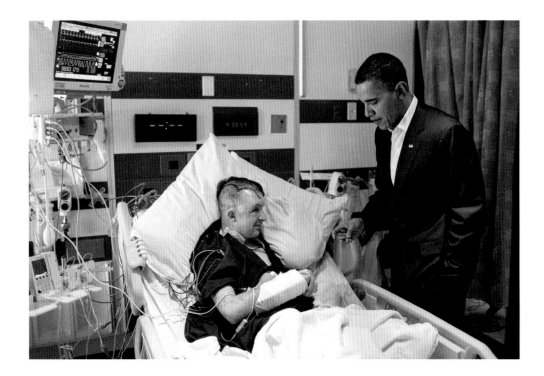

The President had an enduring relationship with Vice President Joe Biden. For eight years, they worked in partnership for the good of the country. And their relationship grew to become closer in the last few years because of the challenges they faced, both personal and political.

Consoling the Vice President after delivering a eulogy for Beau Biden, his son, who had died of brain cancer.
JUNE 6, 2015

Helping the Vice President edit his remarks before he announced that he would not run for President. **OCTOBER 21, 2015**

Surprising the Vice President with the Presidential Medal of Freedom, awarded with distinction. "To know Joe Biden is to know love without pretense, service without self-regard, and to live life fully," the President said during his formal remarks. **JANUARY 12, 2017**

Comforting the Wheeler family in Newtown, Connecticut. Their son Ben had been shot and killed along with 19 other first graders at Sandy Hook Elementary School, on a day that the President later called the worst day of his Presidency.

DECEMBER 16, 2012

Going over his remarks before the memorial service for those killed at Sandy Hook. Two teachers had written a note on the whiteboard: "Dear President Obama, the Newtown community is so thankful that you are coming to help us heal. In times of adversity it is reassuring to know that we have a strong leader to help us recover." The President wrote his response on the board: "You're in our thoughts and prayers."

DECEMBER 16, 2012

Hugging Representative Gabrielle Giffords before his State of the Union address at the U.S. Capitol. It was remarkable to see the Congresswoman smiling and in good spirits, just a year after she had been shot in the head by a gunman in Arizona.

JANUARY 24, 2012

Have Fun

★ ★ ★

Despite the pressures of the job, President Obama also liked to have fun. Sometimes that meant joking around with a staff member or taking five minutes out of the day to entertain a staff member's young child. I also photographed him competing with friends in sports activities; his favorites were basketball and golf. Doing goofball things, like wearing a tiara with some young Girl Scouts or having a fake conversation with some LEGO figures, was always a possibility.

Nicholas Tamarin, 3, aka Spider-Man, had been trick-or-treating with his father, White House aide Nate Tamarin, during an early Halloween celebration at the White House. The President's secretary told Nate to bring his son by the Oval Office. After spending a few minutes with them, the President turned back toward Nicholas and said, "Zap me one more time."

OCTOBER 26, 2012

"Let's race," the President said as he ran down the Colonnade on a chilly afternoon with Denis McDonough's children. They were headed to the ceremony naming their dad the new White House chief of staff.

JANUARY 25, 2013

President Obama joins in with students during a cultural dance performance at Dillingham Middle School in Dillingham, Alaska.

SEPTEMBER 2, 2015

President Obama jokingly looks through a magnifying glass at a student while visiting a pre-kindergarten classroom at the College Heights Early Childhood Learning Center in Decatur, Georgia.

FEBRUARY 14, 2013

Tipping the scales on the unwitting Marvin Nicholson, the President's trip director, while walking through the volleyball locker room at the University of Texas at Austin. For security purposes, we often made circuitous routes through closed-off areas in public buildings.

AUGUST 9, 2010

Playing with Ella Rhodes, daughter of Deputy National Security Advisor
Ben Rhodes, in her elephant costume for Halloween. The President often
encouraged staff members to bring by their young kids for him to meet.
OCTOBER 30, 2015

Goofing around with 6-month-old Talia Neufeld, daughter of departing staff member Adam Neufeld, in the Oval Office.

JUNE 14, 2013

President Obama poses with Girl Scout Troop 2612 from Tulsa, Oklahoma, at the annual White House science fair. The 8-year-old girls—Avery Dodson, Natalie Hurley, Miriam Schaffer, Claire Winton, and Lucy Claire Sharp—are called Brownies. They had just shown the President their exhibit: a LEGO flood-proof bridge project. The fair celebrated the student winners of a broad range of science, technology, engineering, and math (STEM) competitions from across the country.

MAY 27, 2014

Sliding across the counter to pose for a group photo with employees at a Shake Shack in Washington.

MAY 16, 2014

An intense game of one-on-one with personal aide Reggie Love in New York, a few hours after speaking to the United Nations General Assembly. The President was so proud of his blocked shot that he made Reggie sign an enlargement of the picture. Reggie's inscription: "Mr. President, nice block—Reggie Love."

SEPTEMBER 23, 2009

An impromptu hole of golf in street clothes with aides
Joe Paulsen and Marvin Nicholson after the U.S.–ASEAN
summit at Sunnylands, in Rancho Mirage, California.
FEBRUARY 16, 2016

Posing with a boy who had fallen asleep during the Father's Day ice cream social in the State Dining Room of the White House. "Pete—you've got to get a picture of this," the President called out to me. The boy didn't wake up.

JUNE 14, 2013

President Obama fake-chats with a LEGO statue created by artist Nathan Sawaya for the South by South Lawn (SXSL) event at the White House.

OCTOBER 3, 2016

Dream Big Dreams

★ ★ ★

I always thought that President Obama's motto —"dream big dreams"—meant that each of us is capable of achieving great things if given the chance. He instilled in others the belief that we shouldn't disregard anyone because of their circumstances. We should instead encourage people to realize anything is possible with hard work, a good attitude, and someone to help keep them on the right path. I'm confident he will continue to advocate these principles for the rest of his life.

Carlton Philadelphia, a career nonpolitical member of the National Security staff, was leaving the White House to move on to his next post. After posing for a family photo, his youngest son, Jacob, 5, said he had a question. He wanted to know if the President's hair felt just like his. "Why don't you see for yourself," the President replied. He bent over, and Jacob felt the President's head.

MAY 8, 2009

Making sure his tie was straight, moments before walking out to take the oath of office as President of the United States. He may have been nervous inside but didn't show it as he was about to become the 44th President of the United States.

11:29 A.M., JANUARY 20, 2009

The President with the First Lady in a freight elevator at the Washington Convention Center, heading to an inaugural ball. It was chilly, so he draped his jacket over her shoulders.

11:00 P.M., JANUARY 20, 2009

Visiting the new Martin Luther King, Jr. National Memorial, in Washington. The President would speak at its dedication two days later. "Without Dr. King's glorious words," he said, "we might not have had the courage to come as far as we have."

OCTOBER 14, 2011

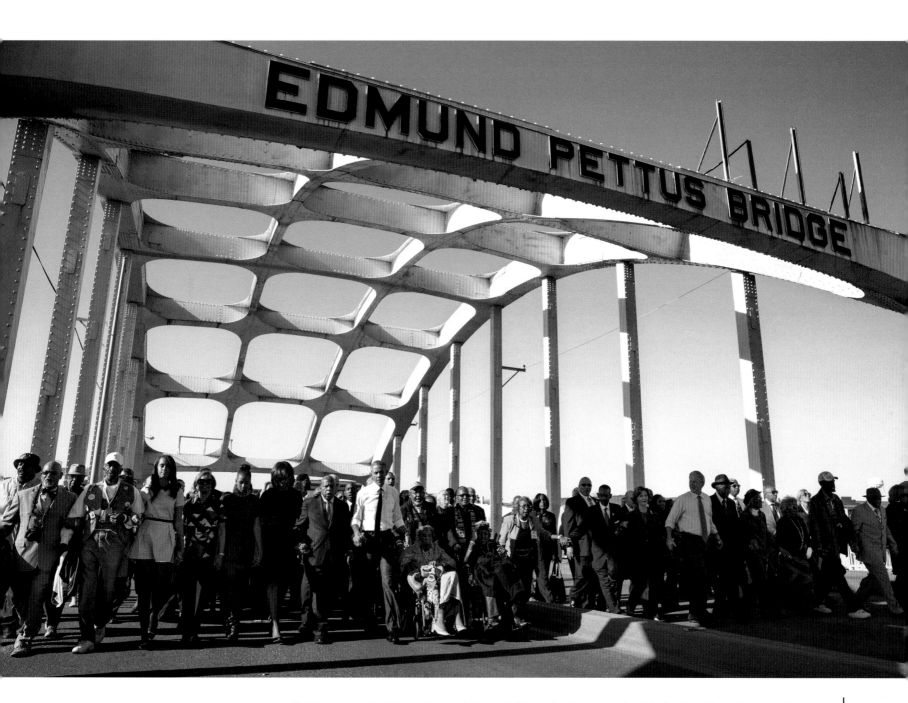

Walking across the Edmund Pettus Bridge with his family, Representative John Lewis of Georgia, former President George W. Bush, former First Lady Laura Bush, and other dignitaries to commemorate the march from Selma to Montgomery, Alabama, 50 years earlier. Representative Lewis had been one of the marchers beaten during a brutal police assault on civil rights demonstrators that helped spur the passage of the Voting Rights Act.

MARCH 7, 2015

On the famed Rosa Parks bus at the Henry
Ford Museum, in Dearborn, Michigan.
The President was at the museum for a
political event and began strolling through
the automobile exhibits. Before I knew
what was happening, he had walked onto
the bus. He looked out the window for
only a few seconds, just long enough for
me to make a couple of pictures.

APRIL 18, 2012

Watching on television in the Roosevelt Room as Congress passed the Affordable Care Act, which eventually helped tens of millions of American people have access to health insurance. President Obama said later that this day meant more to him than being elected President because he had helped so many people by passing this legislation.

MARCH 21, 2010

Walking to the basketball court with a group of mentees after their meeting in the White House. The President met with them on several occasions to provide counsel for their future.

OCTOBER 14, 2014

White House staff gather outside the White House, which was lit in rainbow colors
to celebrate the Supreme Court's decision to uphold same-sex marriage.

JUNE 26, 2015

Greeting new Supreme Court Justice Sonia Sotomayor before her investiture ceremony at the court. Sotomayor became the first Latina Justice in U.S. history, and only the third woman to be appointed.

SEPTEMBER 8, 2009

It was a routine reception, celebrating African American History Month. The President had done dozens of receptions like this in the East Room throughout his Presidency, and they seldom yielded a good photograph. But anticipating that the President would stop to greet Clark Reynolds, 3, I knelt near him in the hope I'd capture their interaction. I ended up making one of my favorite photographs of the Presidency—and it only includes the President's hand. Just after this picture was taken, the President leaned down low to talk with the young boy. Like the photograph of Jacob Philadelphia touching the President's head (see page 81), this one provoked a huge emotional reaction when we posted it on the White House website. We later made a large print for Clark, and the President inscribed it: "Dream big dreams, and work hard to achieve them—you will do great things!"

FEBRUARY 18, 2016

President Obama with 8-month-old Andrew Graham.
FEBRUARY 26, 2015

In memory of Rick McKay and Brandon Lepow